Happy Father's Day, Sweetheart. When I saw this, I knew I needed to give it to you. You are a good man. I'm grateful for you.
Love,
Bonnie

For Roger
the pictures in this book were painted in oil on 3'x5' canvas
with much love
Sarah
(by grandma)

A Poor
Wayfaring Man
of Grief

Text by: James Montgomery
Paintings by: Sarah Merkley

Published by Granite Publishing and Distribution, L.L.C • www.granitebooks.com

ISBN#: 978-1-59936-035-5
Library of Congress Control Number: 2008941561

First printing November 2008. © Copyright 2008 by Granite Publishing and Distribution, L.L.C All rights reserved. No part of this book may be reproduced in any form or by an electronic or mechanical means, including information storage and retrieval systems, without permission in writing from the copyright owners, except for incidental, nonprofit use, or by a reviewer who may quote brief passages in a review.

Printed in China

A Poor Wayfaring Man of Grief

Text by: **James Montgomery**
Paintings by: **Sarah Merkley**

A poor wayfaring Man of grief

Hath often crossed me on my way,

Who sued so humbly for relief

That I could never answer nay.

I had not pow'r to ask his name,
Whereto he went, or whence he came;
Yet there was something in his eye
That won my love; I knew not why.

Once, when my scanty meal was spread,

He entered; not a word he spake,

Just perishing for want of bread.

I gave him all; he blessed it, brake,

And ate, but gave me part again.

Mine was an angel's portion then,

For while I fed with eager haste,

The crust was manna to my taste.

I spied him where a fountain burst

Clear from the rock; his strength was gone.

The heedless water mocked his thirst;

He heard it, saw it hurrying on.

I ran and raised the suff'rer up;

Thrice from the stream he drained my cup,

Dipped and returned it running o'er;

I drank and never thirsted more.

'Twas night; the floods were out; it blew
A winter hurricane aloof.
I heard his voice abroad and flew
To bid him welcome to my roof.

I warmed and clothed and cheered my guest

And laid him on my couch to rest;

Then made the earth my bed, and seemed

In Eden's garden while I dreamed.

Stript, wounded, beaten nigh to death,
I found him by the highway side.
I roused his pulse, brought back his breath,
Revived his spirit, and supplied

Wine, oil, refreshment—he was healed.

I had myself a wound concealed,

But from that hour forgot the smart,

And peace bound up my broken heart.

In pris'n I saw him next, condemned

To meet a traitor's doom at morn.

The tide of lying tongues I stemmed,

And honored him 'mid shame and scorn.

My friendship's utmost zeal to try,

He asked if I for him would die.

The flesh was weak; my blood ran chill,

But my free spirit cried, "I will!"

A poor wayfaring Man of grief
Hath often crossed me on my way,
Who sued so humbly for relief
That I could never answer nay.

I had not pow'r to ask his name,
Whereto he went, or whence he came;
Yet there was something in his eye
That won my love; I knew not why.

Once, when my scanty meal was spread,
He entered; not a word he spake,
Just perishing for want of bread.
I gave him all; he blessed it, brake,

And ate, but gave me part again.
Mine was an angel's portion then,
For while I fed with eager haste,
The crust was manna to my taste.

I spied him where a fountain burst
Clear from the rock; his strength was gone.
The heedless water mocked his thirst;
He heard it, saw it hurrying on.

I ran and raised the suff'rer up;
Thrice from the stream he drained my cup,
Dipped and returned it running o'er;
I drank and never thirsted more.

'Twas night; the floods were out; it blew
A winter hurricane aloof.
I heard his voice abroad and flew
To bid him welcome to my roof.

I warmed and clothed and cheered my guest
And laid him on my couch to rest;
Then made the earth my bed, and seemed
In Eden's garden while I dreamed.

Stript, wounded, beaten nigh to death,
I found him by the highway side.
I roused his pulse, brought back his breath,
Revived his spirit, and supplied

Wine, oil, refreshment—he was healed.
I had myself a wound concealed,
But from that hour forgot the smart,
And peace bound up my broken heart.

In pris'n I saw him next, condemned
To meet a traitor's doom at morn.
The tide of lying tongues I stemmed,
And honored him 'mid shame and scorn.

My friendship's utmost zeal to try,
He asked if I for him would die.
The flesh was weak; my blood ran chill,
But my free spirit cried, "I will!"

Then in a moment to my view
The stranger started from disguise.
The tokens in his hands I knew;
The Savior stood before mine eyes.

He spake, and my poor name he named,
"Of me thou hast not been ashamed.
These deeds shall thy memorial be;
Fear not, thou didst them unto Me."